PRAISE FOR ST. JOHN'S WORT

"It's a treasure of fascinating, authoritative, easy-to-use information that should appeal to everyone."

—Jean Carper, author of
Food: Your Miracle Medicine and *Miracle Cures*

"Norman Rosenthal has given us a book that is exceptionally well informed, enriched by deep scientific scholarship and empathetic clinical skill. Dr. Rosenthal draws on the stories and voices of many hundreds of people who have directly experienced the benefits that St. John's wort can provide. Such a comprehensive and readable book will be a major and unique addition to the literature on herbal remedies."

—Jonathan R. T. Davidson, M.D., Professor of Psychiatry in Behavioral Science, Duke University Medical Center

"Dr. Rosenthal explains what we know about the ancient herbal remedy for depression with the savvy of an experienced psychiatrist and the wit of a good storyteller."

—Dean Hamer, Ph.D., molecular geneticist, coauthor of *The Science of Desire* and *Living with Our Genes*

"Dr. Rosenthal has crafted a masterful blend of lively prose, scientific precision, and clinical wisdom."

—Michael Norden, M.D., author of *Beyond Prozac*

"Norman Rosenthal has done it again—this book is a real winner!"

—Judith Rapoport, M.D., Chief, Child Psychiatry, National Institute of Mental Health, author of *The Boy Who Couldn't Stop Washing*

Also by Norman Rosenthal, M.D.

Winter Blues